To the Students of
Liberty Elementary School

Best Wishes for your success and
happiness & Study hard and you, too,
may become anything you want
to be!

Martha Layne Collins
Governor of Kentucky
1983-1987
September 7, 1991

Best Wishes,
Frances Smith, Ph.D.
9/7/91

The Little Girl Who Grew Up To Be Governor

Stories From The Life Of Martha Layne Collins

Written by Frances Smith, Ph.D.

Illustrated by Pip Pullen

Denham Publishing Company

Lexington Kentucky

This book has been published for the education of young children everywhere.

Jacket Illustration: Pip Pullen
Author's Photograph: Jim Battles
Layout and Design: Group Platinum Advertising
Book Manufacturing: R. R. Donnelley & Sons Company

Published by Denham Publishing Company
P.O. Box 11890, Lexington, Kentucky 40578-1890.
(606) 278-8841
Printed in Mexico

This book is dedicated to
The parents of
Martha Layne Collins,
Mary and Everett Hall,
whose vivid memories and
delightful sense of humor
not only made this book possible
but also a joy to write.

CONTENTS

Introduction

It was very early, but eleven-year-old Martha Layne Hall only had to be called once. Leaping out of bed, she quickly changed into the blue outfit laid out the night before. She was always ready for a new adventure, but this one was special. Her father was taking her to see the president of the United States. It would mean missing a little part of the school day, but that was all right. President Truman was a very important man.

Martha Layne had never heard of a "whistle-stop tour" but that was what President Truman was doing. It meant he was coming to town on a train. When the train stopped, he would come out on a special platform at the end of the last car and talk to the crowd. After a short visit, he would go to the next town and talk to the people there.

When Martha Layne and her father got to the railroad station in Shelbyville, Kentucky, a large group of people were already there. She had never seen them so excited and happy before. Everyone was all dressed up—as if it were Sunday.

"I still can't believe it," one woman said.

"I know," replied her neighbor. "We've never had a president come here before."

Martha Layne listened to the talk. Then she heard a whistle blowing far off in the distance.

Someone yelled, "He's coming! I hear the train."

The crowd tightened around Martha Layne and pressed forward. Before she knew it, grown-ups had closed in on all sides of her. Mr. Hall saw her standing on her tiptoes, straining to look in the direction of the train. She'd never be able to see the president. With one quick sweep she was sitting on his shoulders.

Within minutes, the great iron machine rolled into the station like a proud black giant. Its metal wheels seemed to screech endlessly as they slowed to a painful halt. Finally stopped, the monster hissed billows of steam into the fair October sky. It seemed to command, "Look at *me*!" But in all of it's magnificence, it could not compete with President Truman. Even before he stepped out on the platform, the people cheered and clapped wildly. Some whistled and yelled his name. When they finally saw him, the clapping got even louder. Those close to the train

reached up to shake his hand, he gladly leaned down to them.

Martha Layne watched it all. "How wonderful it must be," she thought, "to be able to make people feel so good, just by coming to see them." She loved the way it

felt—the excitement and anticipation that go with every new adventure or experience.

Little did she know that thirty-five years later an even larger crowd would line the streets of Frankfort to wait for her. Children would miss school. Some would be lifted to the shoulders of their parents so they could see her pass by.

They would ask, "Where is she? When will she be here?"

Finally someone would shout, "Here she comes! See the red coat? She's up there by the driver of the coach."

It was a handsome sight—four proud, prancing horses, stamping their feet and tossing their regal heads, trying to make sure everyone noticed them as they pulled the old, beautiful carriage.

But the attention of the crowd was on the woman waving and smiling from the top of the carriage. The day belonged to Martha Layne Collins—the new governor of Kentucky. And it was a day that marked the beginning of a new adventure for all Kentuckians. They had elected their first woman governor—the only woman governor in the United States at that time.

Now, a governor is almost as important as the president of the United States. The difference is that the president has to help the people in all fifty states, but governors look after those in one state. They work to make sure there are enough jobs in their state. They try to see that everyone is safe, that new roads are built and the old ones fixed, that there are good schools for children, and nice parks to go to.

But the president and governors can't do all these things by themselves. They have to show people how to help. That is why they are called *leaders*.

Martha Layne Collins was a good governor. The people knew she liked them, so they listened when she asked for their help. What they didn't know was she did many of the things it takes to be a good governor even when she was a little girl. From the time she was barely old enough to walk, she worked very hard. She showed courage even when she was scared and was always eager to learn new things. Most of all, she wanted to be helpful.

As you read the stories in this book, look for the things Martha Layne Collins did as a little girl that helped her become governor when she grew up. Then think about the things you love to do. If you are like she was, perhaps you too, will grow up to be governor someday.

Chapter 1
Martha Layne Discovers People

Mary and Everett Hall should have known their daughter was going to have a lot of energy when she decided to come into the world in the middle of the night. It was three o'clock in the morning on December 7, 1936—and it was freezing outside. Cars in those days didn't have good heaters and some of the roads were very bumpy. But the Halls didn't mind the frosty night or the jarring ten-mile drive from Bagdad, Kentucky, to the nearest hospital in Shelbyville. They were ready for the birth of their only child, Martha Layne.

When Mr. Hall heard they had a little blonde-haired, blue-eyed baby girl, it suited him just fine. As for Mrs. Hall, she now had a companion to talk to while she worked. She told Martha Layne all kinds of things. Of course, Martha Layne didn't hear much of it because she slept most of the time.

Bagdad was a small town of only about 250 people. That meant if they decided to go on a vacation together, they could all fit into one jet airplane. But it also meant there were not many things for people to do—except work hard.

Sunday was always a special time. Those who went to church believed it was a day they were supposed to rest and worship. It was also the day most people visited their family and friends.

Martha Layne spent a lot of time at church when she was growing up. Mrs. Hall started taking her when she was two months old. She was very good—usually sleeping quietly in her mother's lap on a soft, fancy, little blue ruffled pillow.

The ladies' Sunday school class enjoyed having her and all went well—until Martha Layne discovered children. From then on, she squirmed and wiggled. She wanted to be with them instead of the ladies.

It all began one Sunday, when a teacher named Sally talked Mrs. Hall into letting her take Martha Layne to the class for five-year-olds. The children crowded around enchanted by their special little visitor. Sally told them if they were very quiet and listened closely to the Sunday school lesson, she would stop a little early so they could play with Martha Layne.

Of course, the children were very good and before long, five little faces were huddled over Martha Layne. They did everything they could think of to get her attention. One put his thumbs in his ears and wiggled his stubby fingers.

Another pushed on her stomach and said, "Hi, little baby"—this upset one little girl in the class. "Doonnn't!" she warned. "You might hurt her."

Most of the class just grinned and watched. When Mrs. Hall came to get Martha Layne, she wondered what in the world was going on.

From the day Sally took Martha Layne to her Sunday school class, Mr. and Mrs. Hall had to share her with lots of people. Someone was always asking to take her home with them and she always wanted to go. It didn't matter if they were young, middle-aged, or older. They were all her friends.

Martha Layne's love of people continued all her life. It was the first sign that she could be governor someday. Good governors have to like all people, and the people have to like them, too.

Chapter 2

The First Journey

Martha Layne never liked being inside the house as much as out-of-doors. Somehow there was always more to do outside.

One afternoon when Martha Layne was about two years old, she must have run out of things to do because she decided to go visiting. But when she got to the gate, it was fastened and she couldn't get out of the yard.

Since the yard was fenced in, Mrs. Hall knew Martha Layne couldn't wander away. Just the same, she checked on her every few minutes. That afternoon when Mrs. Hall looked out the window, her heart nearly stopped beating. Martha Layne was gone! She ran outside and searched all around the house. But it was useless. Martha Layne wasn't there.

Trying to sound calm, she called to her. "Martha Layne?" No answer.

"Where are you, Martha Layne?" Still no answer.

Just then—Mrs. Hall saw that the front gate was wide open. "That can't be," she thought. "I checked it myself when I brought Martha Layne out to play. I know it was hooked."

The thought that someone might have kidnapped Martha Layne never entered Mrs. Hall's mind. People didn't do that sort of thing in a small town like Bagdad. Then she started to wonder if Martha Layne had unlatched the gate herself. It was hard enough for an adult. Surely her little girl hadn't figured out how to get it open! But she had.

Now Mrs. Hall had only one thought and that was to find Martha Layne. Fortunately, the Hall house was surrounded by a big, open field. Mrs. Hall knew there weren't any deep holes or uncovered wells that a small child could fall into. But there was one huge danger just beyond the field—the highway. If Martha Layne wandered onto the highway, she could easily get run over by a car!

Mrs. Hall ran down the dirt path to the main road. Her eyes swept up and down the road, there was no sign of Martha Layne. Mrs. Hall was relieved but puzzled. She *has* to be somewhere. But where? she wondered. Mrs. Hall was so worried that her legs felt weak and she could hardly stand.

"The grocery store," she thought desperately. "Maybe someone at the grocery store has seen her." It was just across the highway. Hurriedly she crossed the road, opened the door and then stopped dead in her tracks. There sat Martha Layne on Miss Frances' lap—having a wonderful time.

Martha Layne could easily see by the look on Mrs. Hall's face that she had done something wrong—*very* wrong. Miss Frances knew it too.

Martha Layne heard Miss Frances plead, "Now, Mama,—don't spank her! She didn't get on the road. I brought her across." Then she looked at Martha Layne. "We were having just the nicest visit while we waited for you—weren't we, Martha Layne?"

Not daring to take her eyes from her mother's face, Martha Layne nodded "uh-huh."

Thanks to Miss Frances, Martha Layne didn't get a spanking. Actually Mrs. Hall didn't much believe in spanking children. She thought there were better ways to make them behave. Her way was either to send Martha Layne to her room or have a little talk with her.

On this particular day, Martha Layne sat in her little chair and Mrs. Hall had a *big* talk with her about how the gate wasn't to be opened and she was never again to leave the yard without permission.

It was important for Martha Layne to listen to her mother when she was little and to do what her parents told her. She didn't understand danger, and they had to keep her safe. But her journey out of the yard showed she could figure out ways to do things even when people didn't think it was possible. And that was good. If she hadn't been able to do more than people thought she could, she could not have become the first woman governor of Kentucky.

Chapter 3
Scared But Hanging In

Growing up in the small town of Bagdad probably helped Martha Layne learn more about how to be a good governor than anything else in her life. Since only a few people lived in Bagdad, they all knew and looked after each other. That meant Martha Layne had lots of good neighbors and friends who showed her how to do things children in big cities didn't get to do. But to do some of them, she had to have courage.

When Martha Layne was about two years old, her parents started letting her go home with Sally after church. There a whole new world opened up because Sally lived on a farm.

Martha Layne liked everything about the farm—riding on the tractor and hay wagon, helping Sally take food to the men working in the fields, playing in the piles of straw—everything. But what fascinated her most were the farm animals.

The first thing Martha Layne always wanted to do when she got to Sally's was go to the barn where the animals lived. But she had to wait until lunch and her nap were over. Sally explained that farming was hard work and she wouldn't be much help if she were hungry and tired.

Martha Layne was usually too excited to go to sleep easily, so Sally read to her at nap time. Martha Layne loved story time and tried to stay awake all the way through. But she never quite made it when they read in the front porch swing. The easy motion of the swing and the quiet, lazy creak of the chains moving back and forth made her so drowsy she couldn't keep her eyes open. Soon she was fast asleep.

After her nap, Martha Layne was ready to help feed the calves. At first she thought calves drank from bottles, just like babies. But Sally didn't use bottles. She had two buckets, each with a long white rubber tube on the side.

Sally explained, "The milk goes in the bucket. And then the calves drink it through this nipple—here on the side."

Martha Layne had never seen a bucket with a nipple before. She stood quietly and watched as Sally filled one bucket with the white, foamy liquid and then the other. Soon Sally announced, "Now we're ready!"

Well, they were almost ready. First, Martha Layne had to climb on Sally's back for the short ride to the pens where the calves were. Even though they were baby calves, they still were much bigger than Martha Layne and could easily step on her. She tightened her grip when Sally warned,

"You're going to have to be very careful, Martha Layne, or you could get squashed." Then looking a bit strange with a bucket of milk in each hand and Martha Layne on her back, Sally headed for the barn.

Once inside, she set the milk and Martha Layne in a feed trough where they would be out of the reach of the calves. Sally knew Martha Layne was eager to help, but first she had to make the calves stand as still as possible. She did this by putting one end of a rope around the calf's neck and then tying the other end to a rail in the stall. Now it was safe for Martha Layne to help her.

Each time Martha Layne stood in front of a calf, she felt a surge of excitement. They were always hungry and giving them food was very important. Sally had to help her because the bucket was too heavy to lift by herself. Together they held it high enough for the calf to reach the nipple. But no matter how steady they were, the nipple kept coming out of the calf's mouth. They tried to make it easy for the wobbly creature, but the weak, sprawled legs often lost their balance. The wet nose would crash into the bucket—pushing it hard against the two people holding it.

"Splat!" went the knobby head.

"Ker-thunk" groaned the bucket. The clumsy calf had missed the nipple and nearly knocked itself out on the bucket. The racket and sloshing milk made Martha Layne flinch and jump back a little. A bit shaken, she knew that whatever "squashing" was, this calf was about to do it to her.

Sally watched the commotion and wondered if Martha Layne would cry and want to go back to the safety of the trough. But instead of crying, she scolded the calf. Putting her hands back on the bucket, Martha Layne looked the calf straight in the eyes. "Stop it!" she said, her fear now turning into anger. "You're being bad!" Sally knew holding that bucket was tough, but Martha Layne refused to be scared away.

One day when they were starting to feed the calves, Martha Layne saw Sally stick her finger down in the milk and then put it in a newborn calf's mouth. Sally said she was teaching the little calf to drink milk from a nipple. As soon as the calf tasted the milk, it started sucking on her finger to get more. Then Sally dripped some milk on the nipple and put the nipple in the calf's mouth. It worked! In no time, the calf sucked the nipple just as it had Sally's finger. Now it could have all the milk it needed.

Of course, Martha Layne had to let the calf suck her finger, too. She knew that a good helper would do whatever Sally did. Martha Layne dipped her finger in the milk just as she had seen Sally do. Then, squinching her eyes almost shut and drawing her shoulders up under her ears as if to brace herself, she timidly put her finger in the calf's eager mouth. What she felt surprised her. Her tongue was smooth, but the calf's tongue felt rough! It didn't hurt, exactly. It was more like a tickly feeling.

Martha Layne's courage came from believing the calves really needed her. She wanted so much to be helpful that she kept on working even when she was afraid. And that is what good leaders must do. If they really want to help their people, they must have lots and lots of courage.

Chapter 4

There *Has* To Be A Way

Martha Layne was about three years old when the family moved next door to the Whitmans. Here she found a new interest—chickens. The Whitmans had a little pen of baby chicks right in their front yard.

Mrs. Whitman was feeding the chickens the first time Martha Layne and Mrs. Hall went to visit her. She took grain from an old bucket, and one handful at a time, scattered the food on the floor of the pen. Martha Layne couldn't take her eyes off of the chickens. They scurried all around, scratching and pecking the floor.

"Tap—tap—ta—tappity—tap—tap—tap." Then they would look up as if to see if anyone was watching them. "Tappity—ta—tappity—tap."

When Mrs. Whitman saw how much Martha Layne enjoyed the chickens, she let her give them some feed. From that time on, Martha Layne just *had* to help feed the chickens.

Once again Martha Layne was a good little helper. She even took her own sand bucket for Mrs. Whitman to put the feed in.

Everything went well except for one thing. Martha Layne could not always get to the chickens when they *needed* her. She was stopped by a giant fence between her yard and the Whitmans', the only way to get to the little pen of baby chicks was by the main road. And Martha Layne had learned a long time ago not to go on the highway without a grown-up. Unfortunately, most of the time, her mother was too busy to take her.

One day Martha Layne stood looking through the fence holding her sand bucket. She knew the chickens were hungry. "There *has* to be a way to feed them!" she fretted. Then she started walking up and down the fence row. "There just *has* to be a way." All at once, she saw it—a tiny gap between two wooden posts just big enough for a small child to squeeze through.

Martha Layne ran inside to get her mother. It was just as she had said. By scrunching between the posts, she could get to the Whitmans' house without going on the forbidden road. Martha Layne anxiously watched her mother's face. Finally Mrs. Hall said, "All right. You may go between the posts to see the chickens—as long as Mrs. Whitman doesn't mind."

Martha Layne knew Mrs. Whitman wouldn't mind. "She needs me to help her," she said. And she was right. Mrs. Whitman did need her help.

Good governors believe that they *must* do certain things, that what they are doing is so important, they can't let anything stop them. But just like Martha Layne, they find ways to do the job without breaking the rules.

Chapter 5

Looking Ahead

One thing all good governors do is look ahead to see what might be needed in the future. Then they try to make sure people will have those things. The first time Martha Layne tried to plan ahead was when she was only four years old.

It started when she saw her daddy do a very strange thing. He stuck a long stick with iron, forklike spikes on it into the ground. The stick was called a *pitchfork*. Martha Layne had seen him use the pitchfork to turn earth over when he planted the garden. But this was different.

Mr. Hall put some earth in an empty coffee can and set it down beside him. Then he picked up clumps of the earth and broke them apart with his hands. The way he looked through the dirt as it fell through his fingers, Martha Layne thought he had lost something.

Then he said. "Ahhh— Now we're getting somewhere," he grinned. "A nice big, fat, juicy one. The fish will *love* you!" When he lifted up his hand for Martha Layne to see, a long, red, wiggly worm was trying desperately to curl around her father's finger.

This was the first Martha Layne had heard about fishing, so she didn't really understand why her daddy needed worms. But that didn't matter. If he needed them, it must be all right. She would help him. Before long, she was watching for worms like they were the most important things in the world.

Some of the worms weren't easy to catch. They'd stick their heads out of a hole. Then when Martha Layne reached for them, they'd pull themselves back down into the earth. She quickly learned to be careful when pulling on the ones that were only halfway out. If she pulled too hard, they broke in half. She decided the best worms were those that slid out on top of the dirt and just laid there waiting for her to pick them up.

Mrs. Hall wondered what her family was doing and went to find them. When Martha Layne saw her coming, she called, "Look Mother, I'm catching worms!" Then she held one up for her to see. But Mrs. Hall wasn't the least bit impressed.

"Oh, Martha Layne—look at you! You're all dirty." Martha Layne hadn't even noticed. Her work was much too important to worry about a little dirt.

Mr. Hall laughed. "Come on, Mary," he teased. "You can help, too."

"Not me," she muttered and turned back toward the house. "You couldn't pay me to touch those slimy things."

The next week, a high school student named Thomas came to dig the garden for Mr. Hall. Of course, Martha Layne watched him work. Suddenly, without saying a word, she took off for the house as fast as her legs could go. Thomas didn't know what had happened. He was afraid something had scared her. But before long, she came back carrying her sand bucket.

"Waaait, Thomas. Waait," she called. Now he was totally bumfuzzled. "What's the matter?" he asked. "What's wrong?"

"Look!" she exclaimed proudly. "It's a worm! My daddy needs this worm. I *have* to catch it for him."

Poor Thomas. He could hardly dig the garden because Martha Layne made him stop every time she saw a worm. "I'll never get through," he sighed. But he did.

And her daddy? Well, Martha Layne had planned for the future. The next time Mr. Hall wanted to go fishing the worms he needed were ready and waiting for him.

Chapter 6

The Helper Gets Help

When Martha Layne was four years old, her family moved to a place where there were even more things to see and do than before. Her new neighbors, Mr. and Mrs. Cox, not only had chickens, they also had hogs, baby pigs, and a big horse named Ol' Nell.

The Coxes were very nice people. They told Martha Layne she could visit their animals any time she wanted. Best of all, she could get there without going on the road.

One afternoon when Martha Layne went to check on the animals, the Coxes weren't at home. She thought that Ol' Nell looked hungry, so she decided to give her some corn.

Mr. Cox always kept his corn in a room inside the big barn called a *corncrib*. It was very old and rickety. Some of the boards were missing from the walls, and the planks in the floor jiggled and creaked each time anyone stepped on them.

When Martha Layne got to the corncrib, she glanced at the mama sows and baby pigs in the pen beside it. Now, animals may not know everything humans know, but most of them have some idea about when they're going to be fed. When the hogs saw Martha Layne, it was about their usual feeding time, so they were sure she was going to feed them. They starting squealing with excitement and shoving and pushing each other to get to where she was.

But Martha Layne wasn't planning on feeding them because they were dangerous and could hurt her. "You'd better let me feed the hogs, Martha Layne," Mr. Cox had warned the first time she helped him. "They're too rough for you. Go over there and feed Ol' Nell. She wouldn't hurt a fly."

Remembering it was all right to feed Ol' Nell, Martha Layne pushed up the wooden handle on the corncrib, opened the door, and went inside. Somehow the room hadn't seemed so dark when she was there with Mr. Cox. Then she noticed the hogs were rubbing and snorting louder and louder—more sure than ever they were going to get fed. Martha Layne decided she wouldn't stay long. Working quickly now, she reached into the huge yellow pile covering the floor for the two ears of corn she wanted to give Ol' Nell.

Suddenly the door swung shut behind her. Now it was *really* dark. Time to leave, thought Martha Layne. But when she pushed on the door, it didn't open. She pushed again—straining hard this time—but it was no use. The door wouldn't budge. The latch had dropped down and to Martha Layne's horror, she was locked in.

Martha Layne tried to be brave, but it was hard. By now, the hogs were digging into the cracks with their greedy snouts—trying to find a way to get in. She could feel their hot breath, and it was getting harder for her to breathe. They knocked and bumped so hard against the flimsy wall, she knew it would break down any minute—and they were going to get her. Finally, she did what any scared kid would do. She yelled and yelled and yelled.

"Mother—come quick! Help me! — Mother— Come—Help!"

Mrs. Hall was in the kitchen talking with Grandmother Hall when she heard the cries for help. Martha Layne had never sounded like this before. She had to be in big trouble. Frightened, Mrs. Hall raced out the door without even stopping to lay down her dish towel.

"I'm coming honey! Hold on, Mother's coming!"

Grandmother Hall hadn't heard Martha Layne so she didn't know what had happened. When she got to the window Mrs. Hall was running straight at the shrubbery.

What is Mary doing? she thought. She's going to hurt herself!

But when Mrs. Hall got to the hedges, it was like she had magic wings. She flew over those bushes like they weren't even there—dress and all. All she could think of was Martha Layne trampled to death by either Ol' Nell or the hogs. If she was going to save her, she couldn't waste any time.

When Mrs. Hall got to the Coxes, Martha Layne wasn't with any of the animals. "Where are you, honey? Tell Mother where you are!"

"Here—over here!" quivered the trapped little voice. But the hogs were making so much noise that Mrs. Hall couldn't hear Martha Layne. She looked everywhere. Finally, she turned in the direction of the corncrib. She thought she saw something move. Looking more closely, she spotted four small fingers wiggling desperately at her through a crack in the corncrib.

This time Martha Layne didn't get a little talk from her mother. Mrs. Hall knew she was just trying to be helpful. The only thing that had upset her was being scared half to death. But she figured Martha Layne was just as scared. *And she was.*

The adventure in the corncrib didn't stop Martha Layne from taking risks when she thought she was doing something helpful. But it taught her a very important lesson. Some jobs are too big and too dangerous to do by yourself. Even the bravest leaders can't make important things happen unless they have help.

Chapter 7

Understanding Changes

One day Mr. Hall said, "Come on, Martha Layne. Let's go see something."

"Something" was a litter of seven newborn puppies. Martha Layne laughed at the way they lost their balance and tripped over each other. Then Mr. Hall surprised her.

"Martha Layne, pick out a puppy and we'll take it home with us." He hadn't gotten the words out his mouth before she swooped down and wrapped her arms around the little brown and white frisky one. She held on to him like someone was going to try and take him away from her. Mr. Hall laughed. There was no way he could change his mind now. The family had just gotten a new member—Spanky.

Soon Spanky and Martha Layne were the best of friends. They went practically everywhere together. If she went inside, he went inside. If she took a nap, he took a nap. She began to think of him as kind of like a little brother or sister.

One day when Martha Layne went inside to get her sand bucket, Spanky didn't follow her. He knew she was getting ready to feed the chickens. It was one of his favorite adventures. He became so excited that he started running circles in the yard. Each trip around the circle was faster and faster and the circles got bigger and bigger. And the bigger they got, the closer he came to the big highway.

Before Spanky knew it, he was on the road. Then a sad thing happened. Spanky got hurt. He ran out so fast, there was no way the car could stop in time.

Martha Layne heard the wheels squeal and Spanky yelp. When she got outside, a man was already running toward the road. It was Tom, a neighbor who lived a few houses away. Spanky was lying on the pavement and he was bleeding. "Spanky!" she yelled.

Carefully, Tom picked Spanky up and carried him to his little owner. At first he didn't know how badly Spanky was hurt, but then he could see he was probably not going to live.

Martha Layne was crying. "Is Spanky going to be all right?" she asked Tom.

"Martha Layne," he said gently. "Spanky is hurt. I'm going to take him home with me where I can take care of him. But I'll bring him back when he feels better." Martha Layne was very upset, but she was glad Tom was going to help her injured puppy.

Each day, Martha Layne asked about Spanky. "Is Spanky well yet? Is he coming home soon?" Finally, her parents told her he wasn't ever going to be able to come home. "Spanky died," they said. "He was hurt so bad that Tom couldn't make him well."

Martha Layne usually didn't ask many questions. But she wanted to know a lot about Spanky. "He broke the rule, didn't he? He got on the road."

"Yes," her parents told her, "and a car hit him." Then they reminded her, "That's why we don't want you going on the road by yourself."

In time, Martha Layne seemed to finally understand and be able to tell people all about Spanky without crying. But she never stopped missing her friend. Her father could see she was lonely.

"Do you miss Spanky?" he asked. Martha Layne nodded her head. "Well, Spanky can't come back," he explained, "but we can get you another dog if you want one."

She hadn't thought about that. "Could we?" she asked.

"I don't see why not," he said.

Soon Martha Layne had a new friend. His name was Fuzzy. And just like Spanky, he did everything she did. But this time, Martha Layne made sure her puppy learned the rule about the road. She was *not* going to let Fuzzy get hit by a car like Spanky did.

It was when Spanky died that Martha Layne learned things can't stay the same. They change—sometimes for good reasons and sometimes for sad reasons. Martha Layne missed Spanky, but by getting another puppy, she didn't have to be sad anymore. Good governors know they can't stop sad things from happening—sometimes even when people follow the rules. But they find ways to help people make things better—just like good parents do.

Chapter 8
Making Things Better

What a good governor wants more than anything is to make life better for people. When Martha Layne was about four years old, she found a way to make "Mr. Le-lon's" life better. His name was really Mr. Leon, but Martha Layne never quite said it correctly.

Mr. Leon lived three houses away from the Halls. He was a quiet man, about 70 years old. Everyone liked him. Martha Layne knew him because he walked a lot by him-self. He loved nature and liked being out-side—just like she did.

Mr. Leon had the habit of meeting some men in the little town at a certain time each day. They sat on a special bench at the store and talked for a long time.

Martha Layne was outside one morning when Mr. Leon went by. "Hi, Mr. Le-lon," she called cheerfully. Surprised, Mr Leon looked toward the yard for the little voice calling his name.

"Hulloo—" he said when he finally saw her. Martha Layne could tell Mr. Leon was pleased because he smiled. She knew he lived by himself and figured he must be lonely. But when he smiled, he didn't look lonely anymore. It came to her that if she smiled and said hi to him every day, she could help make him happy. From that time on, Mr. Leon was very special to Martha Layne.

Since Fuzzy was always at Martha Layne's side, he said hello to Mr. Leon, too. Each morning they ate their breakfast and then hurried out to the end of the sidewalk. Together they sat and waited for him.

Sometimes Martha Layne overslept. "Oh no," she would cry running to the door. "Mr. Le-lon—I've missed Mr. Le-lon."

But Mrs. Hall would stop her. "Come on Martha Layne," she insisted. "Let's put your shoes on and eat your breakfast first."

"Oh Mother, I can't," she pleaded. "I just have to say hi to Mr. Le-lon."

Mrs. Hall never really understood why seeing Mr. Leon every morning meant so much to Martha Layne. Why does Martha Layne think she has to be out there *every* morning, she wondered. She thought it was just foolishness. What she didn't know was Martha Layne believed Mr. Leon *needed* for her to speak to him. She would be letting him down if she weren't there to greet him. So when Mrs. Hall heard Martha Layne's pleas, she couldn't bring herself to say no.

"All right Martha Layne, go on—but hurry up!" she needlessly called after her.

Most of the time Martha Layne hadn't missed Mr. Leon after all.

"Hi, Mr. Le-lon."

"Hullooo, Martha Layne."

Mr. Leon always kept walking. Every once in a while he said, "How are you." It never mattered to Martha Layne that he didn't talk to her. She just wanted him to be happy.

After each greeting, when Martha Layne and Fuzzy turned back toward the house, they looked content—like they had just finished a very important job. And they had. They had made Mr. Leon's life better. That's what good governors do for all the people.

Chapter 9

The Hard Worker

To become the first woman governor of Kentucky, Martha Layne had to work very hard. But that was not a problem, for she had always been a hard worker. Most of the time, she wouldn't even stop to rest until the work was finished. There was one time though, when she wished she had.

It happened when she helped her daddy plow the garden with Ol' Nell. Mr. Hall hitched the wooden plow to the horse's harness. Then he set Martha Layne on Ol' Nell's back. "Hold on tight with your legs or you'll fall off," he cautioned.

Black shields called *blinders* were on the side of Ol' Nell's eyes. This meant she could only see straight ahead of her. Since Ol' Nell couldn't see to turn, it was Martha Layne's job to make sure she went in the right direction.

Riding Ol' Nell was great fun—at first. But after an hour or so, Martha Layne's legs began to hurt. They weren't used to staying in one position so long. She decided to move them around. But when she pulled them up toward her chest, she lost her balance and almost fell off.

She saved herself by quickly pushing her legs back down. I've got to hold on tight, she thought. Unfortunately, there was only one way to stop her legs from aching. She would have to get off of Ol' Nell and walk around. But her daddy wasn't finished yet. So she just had to keep going.

After what seemed like a long time, the plowing was finally done and Martha Layne got down. It was terrible. Her legs were so sore and stiff that she could hardly make them move. She began to wonder if she would be able to walk to the house. That night her parents noticed that she didn't play much. They were surprised when she went to bed early.

The next morning Martha Layne could barely hobble down the stairs. Every step was slow and painful. Finally reaching the bottom, she sat down and rubbed her aching legs. She looked so miserable that Mrs. Hall felt sorry for her. Then, sounding as pitiful as she looked, Martha Layne asked, "Mother, do you reckon Ol' Nell feels this bad, too?"

Mrs. Hall smiled. "Ol' Nell worked hard too, didn't she, honey? But no—I don't think she feels bad. I'm sure she feels just fine." And she did.

Chapter 10

"I Can Do That"

When it was time for Martha Layne to start school, it was like another new adventure. She looked forward to a new place to go, more things to do, and more people to see.

One day her teacher said, "Children, something very special is about to happen. Your parents are coming to visit your room."

At this news, the children became so excited they all started talking at the same time.

"But children," continued the teacher, "our room must look as pretty as it can. I think we need some flowers. Do any of you have flowers you could bring?" The first hand to go up was Martha Layne's.

"I can bring some flowers," she said eagerly.

The teacher smiled and said, "Thank you, Martha Layne."

But when Martha Layne got home from school and told her mother, there was a problem. "Martha Layne," she said in a puzzled voice. "We don't even have one flower in this yard. Where will I get any flowers for you to take?"

Martha Layne wasn't sure. But her class needed flowers, and she just had to help. Her mother was good at figuring out how to do hard things. She would think of something. And she did. Thanks to Miss Abbey and some other good neighbors, Martha Layne got the flowers her class needed. All she had to do was tell them why she needed the flowers and they where happy to help her.

Another day the teacher said, "Boys and girls, we're going to take a field trip and we need some parents to drive their cars." Again Martha Layne's hand was the first in the air. But when she went home with the news, her mother was astonished.

"Martha Layne, you know I don't have the car. Your father takes it to work every morning. How am I supposed to drive?"

Now it may seem wrong that Martha Layne kept getting her mother into things she said she couldn't do. But remember: Martha Layne was sure her mother could find a way to do them. All she had to do was get Mrs. Hall to see how important they were and then she would help. And by being eager to do her part for the group, Martha Layne was a big help to her teacher.

And this is what good governors do. They show the importance of helping—even when some of the people don't think they can at first.

Chapter 11
The Leader

Governors are leaders because they get others to help them do what needs to be done. If people aren't sure what they're doing is the right thing, they won't help. Martha Layne practiced leadership when she talked her parents into helping her, but the first time she persuaded a group to go along with an idea came when she was nine years old. It involved a project that taught her an important lesson.

It was a hot, summer day. Martha Layne and four of her friends sat under a shade tree wishing they could go swimming. But Bagdad didn't have a swimming pool, and there wasn't even one in Shelbyville. The closest pool was more than twenty miles away.

"Think about how nice it would be— jumping in, splashing each other," dreamed Mary Elizabeth.

"I wouldn't even hold my nose," bragged Martha Layne's three-year-old cousin, Cindy.

Martha Layne was listening to the talk when she had an idea. "Hey, why don't we build our own swimming pool?"

"Our own swimming pool?" they chorused.

"Yeah. We can do it. It might take a little while, but we can do it," Martha Layne assured them.

"But where?" Shirley wanted to know.

"How?" asked Patsy.

Martha Layne had it all figured out. They would build it in her backyard. There was plenty of room behind the garden. All they had to do was dig a big hole.

"If we all dig, it won't take us very long," she directed. "But I don't have enough shovels for everyone. Can you find something at your house to dig with?"

By this time, they were excited. "Yeah," they shouted and off they ran toward their homes.

Martha Layne found a shovel and hoe in the smokehouse. She kept the shovel for herself and gave Cindy the hoe. Cindy was really too young to help, but she was so proud to be with her cousin "Marf" that Martha Layne didn't have the heart to hurt her feelings.

"Come on," Martha Layne said to Cindy. "While they're gone, we'll decide where to build the swimming pool." She knew it would have to be pretty big if it was going to hold five people.

"Okay, Marf," said her little shadow with an air of importance.

Soon the others were back with their digging tools. Martha Layne showed them the spot she had chosen and they plunged into their work with great enthusiasm. They chopped and dug, but the ground was so dry and hard, they weren't doing any good. The hoes worked best, but if the girls hit them too hard against ground, the handles stung their arms.

Suddenly Patsy yelled angrily, "Hey, look out! You almost conked me in the head!" Looking sorry, Cindy apologized and promised to be more careful.

At last a small hole began to form in the ground. "It won't be long now," Martha Layne said to the workers. "Just think. We'll have our very own swimming pool right here. Everyone in Bagdad can use it. And it won't cost them any money, either." But just then, her mother came out.

"Hi, girls," she said. "What are you doing?"

"Marf and us are building a swimming pool," Cindy announced proudly.

"Oh—I see," said Mrs. Hall. "Well, are you sure you want to build a swimming pool? They are a lot of trouble you know."

"Oh yes—we're sure," said Mary Elizabeth. "And Martha Layne said we could come swimming anytime we wanted."

"That's fine. But how are you going to keep the water clean?" Mrs. Hall asked. "It

will keep getting dirty and you'll spend all your time trying to get it clean. You don't want to swim in old muddy water, do you?"

The crew looked at Martha Layne. They wanted her to tell Mrs. Hall all about how it could be done.

"Tell her, Marf. Tell her we can do it," said Cindy, tugging at her cousin.

But Martha Layne was thinking it over. She had figured they could dig a big hole, but had forgotten all about the water. "There's no way to get the water clean?" she asked her mother.

"No," came the discouraging reply. "You would have to dip the old water out with a bucket and even then, you couldn't get rid of all the dirt."

Martha Layne realized her mother was right. She hated to say the words, but she had to. "I guess we can't do it."

Her friends couldn't believe what they were hearing. They studied her face to see if there was any chance she would change her mind. Her sad look told them the answer was no.

Disappointed, they picked up their tools and walked away. Their heads were down, but Martha Layne could still hear the voice of a loyal follower: "We could've had our very own swimming pool if Mrs. Hall hadn't stopped us."

The others agreed. "Yeah, if Mrs. Hall hadn't come out—"

Martha Layne had made a mistake, but like all good leaders, she learned something from it. From that time on, she would find out everything she could about a project before she decided to do it—especially if she was going to ask others to help her.

Chapter 12
Martha Layne Collins

When Martha Layne was young, she had no idea she would ever want to be governor one day. But practically everything she did helped her get ready for the job. Whatever there was to learn, she wanted to learn it—whether it was piano, dancing, or swimming. Often her father had to take her to Shelbyville for the lessons.

Shelbyville was a larger town than Bagdad and had more things for Martha Layne to do. So when Martha Layne was thirteen years old and her family moved to Shelbyville, she should have been glad. But she wasn't. She had loved living in Bagdad. All of her friends were there and leaving them was very hard. What made it worse, some of the kids in her class at the new school didn't like her. They called her a "hick" because she had lived in a small town. They said she was "country."

But Martha Layne took an interest in her new life and tried very hard to make new friends. At first she didn't get to do some of the things she wanted to because she was an outsider. But her mother told her not to be upset. "Do well the jobs you are given," she advised, "and later you'll get to do other things." Mrs. Hall's words were easy to follow. Martha Layne had always tried to do a good job.

By the time Martha Layne graduated from high school, she was well liked and was a leader. Her willingness to help her church and school groups in whatever way she could never changed. She always looked for ways to make things better—like being a lifeguard in the summers, and helping to start a teen center so young people would have a place to go. She was in so many clubs and activities, that her parents wondered where she found the energy to do everything.

Martha Layne did two other things in high school that are very important for leaders of a state or country. She studied public speaking and both of the foreign languages taught at her school. Good leaders have to be able to make speeches to large groups and they must care about all people. That includes those from other countries as well as the United States. Martha Layne had always loved people, so it is not surprising she tried to understand more about people from other countries by learning their languages.

When Martha Layne went to college, she studied radio and television. She even had her own radio program. Her idea was to use radio and television to tell people about new inventions and discoveries that would make their lives better. New inventions were a special adventure for Martha Layne. She loved the surprise and excitement of something new and different.

Martha Layne was so good at speaking and showing how to use new inventions that she began to enter and win contests. She liked contests because they made her do her best—not just for herself, but for the groups she belonged to. Most of the contests were hard work, and she learned a lot from them.

Martha Layne also won beauty contests. That means she was chosen to be the Queen of certain special events—like the

Kentucky Derby. Martha Layne felt lucky that people saw her as attractive and always tried to make sure she looked nice.

After college, she married Bill Collins and her name changed from Martha Layne Hall to Martha Layne Collins. She taught school while he studied to become a dentist. Soon he was called Dr. Bill.

They had two children named Steve and Marla, and just like Martha Layne, they enjoyed learning new things.

Steve was like Martha Layne in the way he wanted to go places and be with people. Marla shared her mother's love for animals and swimming. There was nothing Marla liked more than showing her horse named Coe and being a lifeguard.

Martha Layne was glad when Steve and Marla did well in their schoolwork. But she worried about some of the students she taught in her classes. They were getting poor grades on their report cards. Martha Layne knew they would not be able to get a good job someday without an education. So each summer when school was out, she helped them with schoolwork at her home.

From childhood into adulthood Martha Layne looked for ways to do things better. Not all people are like that, but good leaders are.

Chapter 13
The Politician

When Dr. Bill finished dental school and the family moved to Versailles, Kentucky, Martha Layne did as she had always done. She took an interest in everything going on around her. She taught school, helped at church, and joined several clubs that were doing things for the community.

One day a *politician* named Wendell Ford asked Martha Layne to help him campaign for governor. Politicians are people who are paid through taxes to run the government. Some are good and some are not so good—just like it is with all workers.

Good politicians use the government to help as many people at one time as they can. Mr. Ford told Martha Layne that he wanted to help the people of Kentucky have a better life. He sounded like a good politician, so she helped him.

An election *campaign* is a contest where at least two people want the same job. The politicians who win are those able to talk the most people into voting for them. They have to be able to make good speeches and ask people to contribute money so they can afford to talk to a lot of people at one time through television and radio.

Martha Layne enjoyed working in Mr. Ford's campaign. She used everything she had learned about contests, radio and television, and making good speeches. She did such a fine job, other politicians asked her to help them, too. Soon there was too much work and she couldn't be a teacher anymore.

Then the people wanted her to be a politician, too. Martha Layne liked the idea of helping people through the government. But nearly all politicians were men. She wasn't sure if people would vote for her since she was a woman.

The job she wanted was clerk of the Kentucky Court of Appeals. She was interested in the courts because they help people be fair to each other. She knew there would always be arguments between some of the people. But she liked the way the courts helped them keep from hurting each other by

using laws to say who is right and who is wrong. The court tries to make sure people understand the law and follow it. And if someone breaks the law, the court says how the person should be punished.

Martha Layne decided she could be a good politician. But just like Mr. Ford, she had to get people to help with her campaign. Actually she had to win two campaigns. You see, there are two major political parties—the Democratic Party and the Republican Party. Most politicians and voters are either Democrats or Republicans.

First, Martha Layne had to convince Democrats in what is called a *primary* election, that she was the best person for the job. And the Republicans had to pick their best candidate. Then, the Democrat and Republican who win must run against each other in the *general* election.

Most people didn't know Martha Layne had what it took to win campaigns. They didn't think a woman would do well. "Why, she hasn't even run for an office before," some said. "There is no way she can win."

But Martha Layne was a person who loved to meet people and could figure out things nobody thought she could. She had courage and didn't give up easily. Even when she was tired, she worked hard and always looked for better ways to do things. A person like that wins.

Election day came. Now the people would decide who would win. Their choice was Martha Layne—first in the primary election against the other Democrats and then in the general election against the Republican. It was a very exciting time. Now, she was clerk of the Kentucky Court of Appeals.

Martha Layne liked working with the courts. She did a good job and thought of something that hadn't been done of before.

She made a brochure that explained the new Supreme Court to school children.

Then the people wanted Martha Layne to run for an even more important job. They wanted her to be the lieutenant governor. This person helps the governor in the same way the vice-president helps the president. This means she would be the person in charge of the government when the governor was out of the state, or if he became ill or died. The lieutenant governor also stands in front of a big chair in the Senate branch of the government and makes sure the senators follow the rules and take turns when they talk about the laws.

Martha Layne believed she could do many good things for people as lieutenant governor, so she decided to run. Five Democrats ran against her in the primary election—all men. She was helped by a woman named Thelma Stovall who was already lieutenant governor. Mrs. Stovall had proved that a woman could do a good job.

Martha Layne campaigned every day from 6:30 in the morning until midnight, except for Sundays. She worked so hard, the staff traveling with her began to say she was wearing them out. But Martha Layne didn't stop—and it was a good thing. The race was very close. But she did it again. She won against the five Democrats and then she won against the Republican. Now Martha Layne Collins was lieutenant governor of Kentucky.

Martha Layne liked being lieutenant governor more than anything she had ever done. She went to the people to find out what they needed and to ask how she could be of help to them. She spoke at their meetings and helped with ribbon-cutting ceremonies—doing whatever she could to make their events even more special. She asked them to tell her their problems with the government. Then she and her staff listened and tried to find out who could help them.

But as hard as Martha Layne worked to be a good lieutenant governor, not everyone liked her. Some became angry if she didn't help with a law they wanted. It bothered Martha Layne when someone was upset with her, but it didn't stop her from doing what she thought was right. She didn't take sides with any particular group and soon many of those who didn't agree with her had to admit she was fair.

Then the people began to wonder if Martha Layne would be willing to do even more for them.

Chapter 14

Governor Of Kentucky

The people saw that Martha Layne Collins was a good politician. She had come to their towns and schools to find out what they needed. She had gone into coal mines to learn what it was like to work there. She visited older people in nursing homes. And she showed concern for the many people who told her they needed a job.

The people knew and trusted her as their friend. They could tell she wanted to help them, so they asked her to try for a job no woman had ever held. They wanted her to be governor of Kentucky.

And on November 8, 1983, their wish came true. Martha Layne Collins was elected as their next governor—their first woman governor. They cheered and hugged each other. Some even cried with happiness. It was a very proud moment for Kentuckians.

When Martha Layne Collins became governor on December 13, 1983, many things happened.

She rode in a long parade on a beautiful coach drawn by four powerful Canadian horses. People lined the streets for miles to show their new governor they were proud of her.

There was a special ceremony called an inauguration. She placed her hand on three Bibles held by Steve and Marla and solemnly promised to help the people of Kentucky have a better life.

Everyone dressed up for the Inaugural Ball. They watched their new governor descend a long, white marble staircase and admired her—saying she looked like a queen.

Her new home was a beautiful mansion. She invited thousands of people to come to see her.

She lived there with Dr. Bill, Steve and his wife Diane, Marla, and her dogs—Jinx and Riley— and her cat, Peppy.

She had a fine, hard working staff and a big office with flags in it and lots of papers to read and sign.

She made many speeches. Sometimes she flew to them in a helicopter named Sikorsky.

She helped children by getting more money for their schools and creating new adventures for them—like the Bluegrass Olympics, the Governor's Scholastic Cup and School for the Arts. She went to special performances by children and afterward, they would run to *their* governor—waving their arms and yelling, "Governor! Governor!" And she would speak to every one of them before she left—no matter how long it took.

She worked with the people in business and industry and brought more jobs to Kentucky than anyone ever thought possible for her small state.

Her love of all people took her to countries like England, France, West Germany Japan, Korea, China, and Switzerland, where she made many new friends for Kentucky.

The president of the United States invited her to visit the White House.

She even had lunch in Buckingham Palace with Queen Elizabeth, the queen of England.

It was all very, very exciting. Martha Layne Collins had kept her promise to help the people of Kentucky have a better life. Just think, it all started with a courageous, adventurous little girl who loved people and, more than anything else, just *had* to be helpful.